I Do Not Exist

and Neither Do You!

Realizing the Essence of Being

By G. Tyler Wright

Table of Contents

1   The Field of I

I do not exist. There is no me, no mine, no I. You do not exist either.

Obviously this is not the way most of us experience life; nonetheless it is true.

The bodies and minds of the world exist in a field of I. This field is everywhere and permeates everything and everyone. This field gives everyone the illusion of being an individual person, but in truth only the field is the I. All the bodies and minds are nothing more than movements in the field.

We happen: we have no volition. Everything we think is because of the accumulation of energy, experience, and beliefs we have in each moment. Everything we do just happens, a product of our past knowledge, the world around us, and the interaction of the two.

The field of I gives us the feeling of self. Without this field, we are just bodies and minds moving and doing like robots running a program. This field gives us the illusion of having a life and a purpose. It allows us to think we are an important part of this creation. In turn the minds give the field of I thought. This means the field of I can examine itself from a limited perspective using the mind inside of this creation. The bodies allow the field of I to do, instead of just being.

Is this radical nonsense? No, it is actually our daily life experience, but we do not have the correct perspective to see it this way. We are born and immediately taught that we are this individual by others who were indoctrinated into this same misunderstanding at their birth. We live in societies that support this illusion. We speak languages that strengthen this belief. But the monkeys got it wrong! Or maybe the most recent ancestor isn't to blame. Maybe it goes back millions of years to the very first ancestor who thought or saw or even felt separate from its surroundings.

With a set of neurons complicated enough to feel, the field of I was born. The belief that I exist, a something with a small separate location different from the others around me came into existence with a certain level of complication of the brain. There was not a complex thought process at that time, just the feeling of separate identity. This was taught to the next and the next and when we evolved into more and more conscious animals, it was one of the basic beliefs that went unquestioned, and it was taught and refined throughout evolutionary history.

So today we find ourselves with a language and a belief system so ingrained and pervasive that to even form the question of such a basic tenet of our lives seems ludicrous. Of course I exist, of

course I am a person, you say. You're nuts,

some may also say. The truth is you are right! I

am nuts. Inside of this perspective of

personhood in which we are all born and raised

there does not seem to be a basis for

questioning this foundation of life. But in the

moment we get a glimpse of another

perspective, the old one falls away.

2   The Search for Freedom

As long as life is normal, filled with family,

friends, job, and our favorite screen, we do not

see the possibility of anything more. Despite

this lulling into complacency that life

accomplishes, something deep inside of us all

yearns for this knowing, which is why so many

of us drink, smoke, do drugs, or seek various

thrills. Deep inside at a place we do not

consciously connect with, we know there is

something else, something better and more real

than what we know now. We don't really know

how to connect with it, so we do something

that we have stumbled upon in the past which

11

gave us a taste of the feeling of freedom from

this misunderstanding we call our place in life.

Why drink or smoke or any of the many other

activities that we do? For a moment they

disconnect the mind from the field of I.

While the vices of life can do this for us, the

same can be seen with the achievements and

highpoints that others strive for. When we are

in the zone in a sport or playing music or

excelling at numerous other activities, we again

let go of the mind and allow ourselves to

become what we really are when we let go of

this misunderstanding that so permeates our

entire existence. And when we are free from

the belief of being a person, even for a fleeting

12

moment, we experience life as it was meant to be lived.

We know ourselves in this tiny moment not as a body with a mind and a past and a life, but as existence itself unattached from all, not needing anything, not wanting anything, not expected to do anything or achieve anything, but just pure, free beingness. This is a feeling that is so new and intoxicating while at the same time so old a familiar that we yearn to return to it again and again, and we do whatever it was that took us there in the first place in the belief that this is our personal key to experiencing bliss.

For some, this search for the feeling of freedom drives their bodies to destruction, and for others this quest drives them to achievement and greatness in a particular endeavor, but for all it still only dances around the truth of what is the ultimate driver deep within. You do not exist.

3   Who Are You?

The doing you think you do is just the

happening authored by creation. You are the

intimate feeling of being that you touch when

you get that high through your drug or activity

of choice. You are that I we all share, that the

paucity of language cannot begin to enunciate.

You are that feeling of beingness we all strive to

feel and live in tune with.

This body and this mind are not you. They are

on you, but they are not you. The real you

permeates the body you now believe you are

and the mind you believe you have. You are so

free that modern science cannot touch or see or

define you. You are so free that words cannot

describe you and feelings cannot touch your essence. Your freedom is such that a whole universe of people, places, and glorious galactic things cannot begin to know your incredible being.

Maybe you are the so called dark energy of physics. Maybe you are the spirit of various religions. Maybe even you are the God that religions teach you to adore.

In the stillness of that space where the true you exists, beyond the mind and the body, you can begin to experience what/who you truly are. Then you are not tied to your drug or activity of choice anymore. Then you are free to live in the knowledge of the truth of your being, in

constant connection with it. You can enjoy
yourself in the foreground of the body/mind
experience, or in the background while doing
some activity.

You know that whatever you do, does not take
you closer or further from what you really are.
You see that what you mistook as your key to
bliss was really only one of an infinite variety of
ways for the mind to realize there was an
immense, blissful background of silent, amazing
beingness right behind it always, just waiting to
be recognized.

Once seen and understood, it never goes away.
Once realized, it is always the true self, never to
be mistaken again.

4   Beginning the Journey to Realization

So if you are still with me on this journey of self-discovery, you must be able to see on some level the immense misunderstanding that the human race lives inside. You must also see the incredible existence that lives on the other side of understanding. So you have to wonder, how do I get there? How do I change my understanding to know my true self?

The trip from ignorance to knowledge is as short as the space between your next breath, or as long as the rest of your life. Some who have read this or heard these thoughts have already

gotten it and are now and forevermore in touch

with their true I and have let go of their former

mistaken identification with their body and

mind. Some who are reading this or who have

touched this knowledge will think about it,

doubt it, wish to believe it or something in-

between. They will spend their lifetime wishing

for an awakening that will never come because

of previous beliefs about how that awakening

should look, and what that experience of

beingness should feel like. They will spend a

lifetime trying to find an experience in the

world that matches their preconceived beliefs,

even as the reality of what they are sits right

beside them, forever just out of reach.

If you want to hold onto your limited belief of

being a person, a body with a mind and all that

goes along with that, then enjoy the illusion,

and ignore the inner yearning to know more.

If you are ready to let go of previous beliefs and

fly free to the truth of who you are, if you are

ready to experience your happiness and bliss

within, then come along and experience the

essence we all share.

I Do Not Exist and Neither Do You!

5   Right Understanding

The first thing to understand is the hardest of

all. You do not exist. And if you do not exist,

then there is no choice. There is no you to do

anything, no you to think anything, no you to be

you. There is only being. And this being has no

care or knowledge about the you that does not

exist, or of the world that you do not exist in.

Thought is for form. The beingness that we are

is beyond form and thought and caring and

crying and loving and any other concept our

minds can conceive of and experience. What we

are is an isness that transcends every concept in

23

this world. What we are, in a sense, uses the things of the world to become people and places and things. It creates all that exists and supports all that exists.

It is imperative to understand who we are and to ingrain this understanding deep within. To do this, we must begin to see this in our everyday lives. We do this by changing how we approach the events of our lives. This change requires us to see things from the new perspective of beingness which is beyond all of this creation. We must accept and observe the happenings of life, instead of using the mind to pretend to take part in the happening. We must watch more, and believe we are controlling less. We most definitely must stop using the mind to criticize all that happens around us, and instead understand that the entirety of creation has conspired to make every moment you and everyone else experiences exactly the way it is.

There are no exceptions to this order of life. Nothing sneaks in and happens without the universe making it happen. Once we understand and accept this truth as the operational fact of life, we can begin to let go of the belief that we must do this or accomplish that in order to have a good life.

I Do Not Exist and Neither Do You!

6   Making the Shift

This belief in doing is an immense pressure we place on top of our being every single day, and when we remove it, the feeling of freedom is palpable. When we let the universe be as it already is, when we let creation do what it is planning to do already, without your volitional help, then we become much more in tune with the flow of this existence. When we watch without commenting or complaining or judging, but instead observe with only acceptance, we find ourselves more in touch with our essence. Finally, when we can begin not only to accept, but to embrace and celebrate the happening,

27

whatever it may be, then we are opening

ourselves to experiencing the bliss that lies

behind each moment of creation.

When we greet the moments of life with a smile

and the understanding that this is what the

entire universe has literally placed in front of

itself at the point that you call me, your

perspective has shifted, and you are ready to

experience your being as the real part of your

day. As you do this, the things of your life

become less important, and the feeling of

beingness becomes more primary in your

awareness. You stop looking for the things of

your life to give you satisfaction and joy, but

instead see that your joy and bliss are always

there as the feeling of being, which has always

been there, behind all and throughout all, always. In a sense you stop looking in other people's backpacks for your gold, and instead open your own backpack to see your treasure has always been with you. You realize your happiness is not in the events of life, but it is in the life itself. You don't look outside, searching for something to make you smile; you smile because the feeling inside exists, and you are now connected to it with the sense of self recognition.

This can happen as an incredible transformation experience, a small shift in consciousness or anything in-between, depending on how creation has chosen to experience it through the space formerly known as you. The universe

29

could literally open up to your being and you

could know yourself as one with all existence,

or you could find yourself entertaining a new

thought, the final piece of understanding, and

you would say, oh yeah. Or anything in

between. The only important aspect of any real

awakening is that the shift to experiencing the

inner feeling as real, permanent, and all-

pervasive and as your self has occurred.

The feeling and your identification with it gets

stronger as you live with it every day. One day

you look up you see that no, I do not exist. I

really never existed, and I now live in a world in

which no one exists, yet the play of existence

continues. And the play is good, entertaining,

and the part that creation now has you playing

is perfect, not for you, but for the universal

creation living in and as you, ultimately known

as field of being.

I Do Not Exist and Neither Do You!

7   Changing the Way We Think

So how do you go about changing a belief that has been so ingrained in society as to predate society? Amazingly, you can use the same tool that currently holds you captive, albeit in a different way and on a different level. The mind is the tool that has accepted the teachings, and the mind is the tool that will need to let go of the teaching too.

The surest way for the mind to see its predicament is to be open to other possibilities, and then to use its awareness, which is at a level beyond thought, to root out the misunderstandings that most of us live under.

Starting this inquiry means you have an acceptable level of openness to new possibilities, so getting this far means that you can possibly imagine a perspective exists that is different from what you currently believe. From here, you must learn to use consciousness in a different manner than most societies teach.

Usually from a very early age we are taught to think about everything. We are taught that it is useful to have words moving in our minds and to picture what would happen in a certain situation if we do or do not perform a certain action. We equate thinking with good and not thinking with bad. After a few years of this indoctrination, we believe that the only state the mind can exist in is that of thinking, and we do not even believe that it is possible to stop thought. In fact we don't want to stop thinking as it seems to be both undesirable and unnatural. What would I do if I wasn't thinking, a frantic thinker would ask.

The space beyond thought is where we can learn about who we really are, and we can get a glimpse of our true potential. The state of thinking is useful when we need to classify various things and activities and people in our lives. It has its place in the world as we know it, but it is limiting.

Thinking can only state how something appears in a given moment at a specific perspective. It is very good at that, but it does not see its limitations. When a thought is formed, it calcifies pretty quickly, meaning it becomes accepted and real for the thinker moments after it has been formed. It becomes connected to other thoughts and fits neatly like a piece in a puzzle. Each thought is not put in its place with the caveat that what is thought here -the classification or box that has just been created- is only relatively true. It is not understood to be true and of value when seen from the place it has just been seen from. It is not accepted to be useful mainly to the mind which formed the thought using the life experiences that it holds.

If we really began to understand the truth of

the boxes we create, we would not hold onto

them nearly as tightly as we do, and we would

be much more open to new information when it

arrives.

So thinking has a use, but it is not the only

useful state that the mind can experience.

Thinking is not so useful when it comes to

enjoying life. It can get in the way when we are

taking in something beautiful. To think about a

vista as it opens in front of us, is to try and

classify it instead of experiencing it. It is much

like the mind believes it is a reporter, and must

describe its life to an imagined audience. When

we experience love, we do not need the words

in the mind. When we are in need of swift

action, excessive thinking and categorizing only get in the way of spontaneous action.

We can see that there are many moments in life when we do not think, and thinking is not the best approach. It is the same with understanding and experiencing who we really are. To do so requires us to let the mind move to a place we usually do not take it: to stillness.

When we reduce thinking to a single thought, we are better able to observe the space that exists around the thought. We can see that each word in our mind in a given moment of thinking is never all there is. When we reduce thought to one word at a time, one well-observed word at a time, we can see that there is a stillness behind it, beside it, and even in front of it. Then we can also begin to notice that this space is a lot larger than the word that sits hanging in the dark silence that exists between each thought.

When we can see thought through this new perspective, truly watching each thought and feeling the space around each word, we can also see that the previously unobserved desire for the continuation of thought subsides. We are not quite as compelled to move the thought stream forward to completion. And this is key.

Once we are not as compelled to think, we begin to see that we have control over thinking. We are not the thinker, but we are the watcher of the thoughts. Each thought is not a part of us, and we are not bound to continue watching it if we do not choose to do so. Thinking is not who we are and we are not the owner or creator of the thoughts. We have the capacity to watch it, but we also have the ability to stop watching when we want. We are not the slave of thought, and we begin to master our true relationship with it when we see we can pay more attention to the space around a thought than to the thought whenever we choose.

The key to beginning to experience true freedom is, simply put, stop thinking so much, and start savoring the spaces in-between each thought.

8   Recognizing the Space

Once you start to recognize the space of

awareness between each thought, you begin to

see it is everywhere. Much like when you think

of a color or a type of car, then you seem to see

it everywhere, the same is true of the stillness

within. Once you recognize its face, you see that

it is all around you. Everywhere you look, you

can see that same feeling of peace and still,

vibrant energy. It is there when you look at a

tree, or a mountain in the distance, or a child's

face smiling up at you. You can observe them all

inside of the stillness that begins to hint at your

true essence within.

More formally, if this is the approach that best suits you, you can sit still in a chair, close your eyes, and begin to watch your breath as you breathe in and out. Or pay total attention to the heartbeat inside your body, keeping your full focus on each rhythmic beat. Bring your awareness back to your breath or your heartbeat when it wanders. Or use one word of your choice – like Om, or Being- to focus thought to a single point, repeating it with each breath. Sitting like this for ten or twenty minutes each day will get you into the habit of not thinking, and actually not minding not thinking. After a while, you will start to enjoy the space you create every day, and look forward to feeling the peace, joy and, inner happiness it opens you to experience. Sitting with this focus will introduce you to the space of silence that is in your body and your mind which you may have only fleetingly noticed before.

At this point you begin to take this practice beyond your time of sitting. Once you see the inner space exists inside your body and mind, you will see that it does not end there. In fact the extent of your inner stillness is limited only by your understanding. Once you feel it and know what it feels like, when you look at that tree, or the blades of grass blowing in the breeze, you will see that the same feeling you felt inside your body can be felt when you eliminate the difference between you and what you see.

You can allow your awareness of that sense of stillness to reach out to the blowing grass, and you will see that it has been there all along, waiting for you to understand it. You can know the feeling in the clouds as they pass overhead, and again, you recognize it as the exact same feeling you know from communing with it inside when your attention is within your body. That feeling you will come to understand as your real being is not limited by where your body is, but only by where you allow your consciousness to expand to.

Most wonderfully, you can also see it within others. You can stare into your beloved's eyes and feel that same feeling that is your own self deep within. It is amazing to experience that who you thought yourself to be is no different from the one you love in this world. You look at your family and your close friends, and it is easy to recognize that still space of your being inside each one of them. Then you can take it to the streets and realize that even strangers you have never seen before and will never see again also share that essence of your beingness as their own, deep within. You can even visit places of worship and regardless of denomination, again experience that peace in the being of the one being worshipped.

Then you understand that the background and sustenance of each and every person, every place and everything is surrounded and permeated by your own personal, universal experience of being. It goes beyond your thought to the essence of awareness beyond thought. The root of your being is not only you but all.

As you read these words and hear them in your mind, do not be surprised if they transport your awareness into itself. When you talk about the silent space of being, when you hear about it, the vibration of the thought is able to do this for you. Much like how it is easier to see the stillness in your beloved one than it is to see it in a stranger, as least while you are becoming acquainted with it, the power of this conversation pulls you toward this stillness, allowing you to recognize it in a much stronger way than when one talks about football.

Both can pull you within, but the attunement you have to your loved one is greater than to a stranger much like your attunement to your being is more powerful than your attunement to football. Basically it is easier to allow yourself to see yourself in a loved one before you see yourself in a stranger. You can feel your essence in these words before you can feel them in words on a different topic. In the end, they are in all people and all words, and when you know the feeling intimately, you experience it in all people and all conversations.

It comes down to what we allow ourselves to accept as triggers leading to the space within. When we speak of God, some of us appreciate the thought, others do not. The same is true of other words like universe, creation and being.

When we sit in a church, some of us have an affinity for it and some do not. Some may find their bodies swaying, appreciating the stillness – the spirit within- and some do not. The music will touch some of us, and for others an old song on the radio will do just as much if not more to bring about a glorious feeling. It is all about how we allow ourselves to feel this feeling that exists inside all at all times.

You can decide to accept that it is everywhere

and fall in love for a moment with a stranger

sitting across from you on the bus. Or with the

bus itself, for that matter. With an expanded

understanding of who you are and what your

inner space really is, you see the choice to

experience it whenever and wherever is yours.

I Do Not Exist and Neither Do You!

9   Seeing the Nature of the Mind

How does the mind end up in a trap like this,

you may wonder. If all of this is true, then why

isn't it well known, why don't we hear about it

on the news, or at least in church? Why isn't it a

major study of philosophy?

The truth is the same as using the eye to see the

eye. Most of us spend so much time looking

through our eyes, that studying the tool of sight

does not hold a lot of interest or even make a

lot of sense. As long as your eyes work, you use

them, you don't question them. Or as long as

51

you are able to breath, you don't worry about your lungs too much.

Basically we take the mind and its functioning for granted. It is such a basic part of our lives, such a foundational tool, that we forget that it is just that: a tool. It is a tool we use, but it is not who we are. It has thoughts about the world around us and our current situation, and it thinks about various pieces of life, forming opinions and solidifying belief structures, but it is really only the movement of creation at a given place, in a specific moment. It is not you.

A wonderful way to see the mind is to watch it like you would watch clouds floating in the sky overhead, blown by a gentle breeze on a warm summer day. They come out of nowhere, drift

calmly past you, changing shape and usually

dissipating, then they are gone. The same is

exactly true of every thought: it comes from

nowhere, floats into your awareness, the

conscious field that you are watching. It

changes shape, develops, then it is done and

gone. When you can watch it in an unattached

way, just like you observe a cloud, then you will

see your real relationship to each thought.

Most of us do not watch clouds wishing they

would do this or that, wanting them to do a

specific thing and getting attached to their

existence. We do not need for a cloud to go

from one end of the sky to the other, but we

just let it be as it is. When we stop being so

attached to each thought and instead take as

much care for them as we do clouds in the sky,

then we are free from their attractive clutches.

Then we allow thought to return to its rightful

place as a tool that we use as needed, one that

is put down when its usefulness comes to an

end.

Normally we allow random thoughts to go

around in our minds, and we identify with them

as our own and as how we think. When they are

truly no more important than clouds, and no

less random many times, we still use each one

to shape who we believe ourselves to be, to

show how we think, and to rank what we find

important in life.

This unobserved mind is of the nature of a child. It needs to be continually watched. Its conclusions must be praised. A train of thought must be carried from beginning to end. Each thought is so important that we allow them to keep us from living life as it is happening. Instead of enjoying a moment, we catalog it moments after it occurs. We don't live as much as we chronicle the life we experience through our thoughts about it.

I Do Not Exist and Neither Do You!

10 Changing Your Relationship to Thought

With your newfound relationship with the space of consciousness behind thought, try watching your thinking. Instead of following it, identifying with it and fueling it, just watch it. Decide that no thought is so important that you should lose your awareness of watching it, then just observe. When you do this you will find that thought does not have the power that it once had to suck you into it. You will observe other things about the quality of your thoughts as well.

Another exercise is to watch a train of thought and then consciously stop thinking it. Do not follow the train to its station. Let the thought just stop, like an opinion ended in mid-sentence. Just don't give getting to the conclusion any energy. See how this feels.

Since you have probably never done this before, it will probably be hard. All your life it has been as if each thought expects to be carried to its conclusion. Thought feels entitled to be completed every time. To stop this pattern, even once, requires a tremendous effort. The energy of the thought hangs there, yearning for the thought to be finished, but when it finally really sees that a thought will not be finished, there is a release of energy that goes back into

58

the observing consciousness. It is like an inner

burst of ahh. If you keep this practice up for

some time, again you will eventually notice

something interesting.

Thought really wants to be used. Whether it is a

useful one, or an idle one, it wants to be

formed, watched and allowed its time on the

plane of your mind. When it clearly sees it is

under attack, when it understands that you

have a new perspective on thought, one that

does not automatically let every thought have

its moment in the sun of your consciousness,

thought gets smart. Whereas before you

watched your thoughts, you might find yourself

in deep contemplation about the way one co-

worker talks to another, now your mind knows

it cannot offer such a trivial thought because it will not fly. Instead it starts musing on the meaning of life, or it spontaneously realizes how to solve a problem you had forgotten you were working on. It gives you a higher quality thought. Creativity becomes much more alive when you respect the tool that is the mind enough to stop it from wasting itself on just any thought.

Now you can stop here and enjoy the higher quality thoughts, or you can smile and watch the mind, knowing its game. When you approach this watching of thoughts with the belief that there is no thought more useful than the stillness beyond thought, and then stick to it, you will find there is still another prize

waiting for you: bliss.

11   The Bliss Beyond Thought

Yes, that's right, when you allow the mind to

subside and the awareness that it is made of

becomes important enough to watch and

appreciate, then you find yourself diving deeper

into the feeling of the stillness. The deeper you

go, the better the feeling. At first it may be

unfamiliar to go so deep into stillness, but as

you do, you feel the energy of consciousness

surrounding you. You feel the bliss of being that

your true essence has always been.

When you can see this feeling as limitless, going beyond your body and out to your surroundings and beyond, you will also feel the growing bliss surrounding you and overwhelming you. Once again, your belief and level of acceptance of this new experience is your only limit.

The feeling of I that you previously believed to be attached to your body and mind can now be seen for what it really is. The mind is an "I" detector. In the field of being in which we live, it is a complex enough organization of molecules that it senses the feeling of being. It interprets that feeling as an I or a self, and appropriates that self to be its own. The mind limits the feeling of I to find it inside its body and mind. I am only this mind, complete with all the thoughts it thinks, and this body, believes the mind. Of all the things it thinks about, the "I" sensing mind never turns to think of what it is doing with that feeling of I that it creates, interprets, limits, and steals.

The enlightened mind can instead see that this feeling exists everywhere. The misunderstanding mind interprets it as I, but this feeling is deeper than even the feeling of I. It is in actuality the beingness of all of creation. The unenlightened mind does a disservice to think of the I as an individual. Yes, this interpretation of this universal feeling as an individual is part of the game that creation is playing, but that does not mean you should always be immersed in this game.

12   Letting Go of Doing

Creation is an organization of being in motion. It could be stated as Creation, or creation, depending on your preference, although it is universal (or multiversal), not personal. It started on its own and moves along with no more volition than the initial movement of being in itself. Being interacts with itself, it grows in complexity, and it has even come to the point now where a limited aspect of itself can be self-aware.

We believe we are performing actions, doing things, in charge of activities, and responsible for good works, when in reality we are really not doing anything. What we all are, at our essence, does not have a body or mind, so it cannot do anything. We can only be. Beingness can only be. We appreciate and enjoy this creation through the body and mind that we find ourselves intimately experiencing, but we are not this. So even this search that we are on to better know ourselves, is not being done by us. The experiments of the mind are not being done by us. None of it is our personal doing; it is the flow of creation playing with itself as a myriad of individuals.

There is one source of all, and that as the aspect of awareness is our interface with this world. Even as we, as beingness are truly beyond all of this, we have the illusion of experiencing it. As beingness, that is all we are. In truth we know only ourselves as being, and this world has no existence to us. The absolute being knows only the absolute.

Our practical experience of a living awareness in a body is a bit different though. As mindless, body-less being, we do nothing; as the motive force throughout all creation, we do everything. Perspective is key.

When the mind is free of its eternal conversation, then the awareness behind it can take over. Suddenly you find yourself experiencing your body, feeling the wind on your arms, hearing the rocks crunching beneath

69

your feet, and watching the trees swaying in the breeze. Life courses through this body instead of around the categorizing entity the mind would have you be. You are no longer struggling to accomplish and do something, but are instead in the flow of being as being.

13   The Absolute

Another way to see it, another perspective, if

you will, is that you are emptiness or space

itself. You are the dark energy of the universe

and all of the matter in the multiverse flows

through you at the speed of a galaxy. You are

the background or the screen and all of creation

passes over you. For a moment, as the play

dances across the screen, a part of the screen

becomes alive. A part of the space that creation

passes through is enlivened by the actions

appearing on it as it lives for a split second

before creation passes through to the next

space, the next part of the screen. Dark energy

knows life, before returning to its absolute

state. With the play moving off its screen, the

beingness is once again itself, unencumbered by

the movement of being upon itself. Much like

the ripples of foam on the surface of the ocean,

there is coming and going, creation and

dissolution without volition, purpose, or care.

But this is a state that the mind cannot

understand or experience. Some call it the

Absolute, and it is basically a black box to those

of us with bodies and minds. The mind can only

speculate with this limited language and

experience as to what that space really feels like

to itself, although the feeling of bliss within the

depths of still, vibrant energy experienced at

times of silent communion with inner peace

gives a fair hint of the possibilities.

For our purposes it is best to continue along,

allowing the universe to move through us as us,

and to enjoy the show. Even if we cannot stop

thinking that we are doing, we can stop

believing it. If the creation wants to stop

moving through you, if it wants to stop

pretending you are the doer, it will. And it will

because the totality of the universal motion

throughout all of time and space has conspired

to make it happen like that in this moment. And

if it continues to use you as someone who

knows the truth, yet continues to play a

seemingly mundane role in this galactic show,

then that is what you will experience. There

73

may be multiverses with every choice played

out, and an infinite number of playwright's

stories being told, but the one we experience

here and now was written at the very beginning

of this universe's time.

14   Letting Life Happen

It would be great to say that now you

understand there is nothing the real you can do,

there is also nothing that the real you can or

should be stressed or worried about, but since

the real you cannot even stress or worry,

there's no problem. But even then, there is not

a you to have a problem, or to control any of

the above. The limited you will have the

experience of worry as long as that is how the

universe intends to experience itself at the

point of your body and mind. When the

accumulated understanding and belief and

energy, at the place where you are physically

75

experiencing yourself, comes to express itself

without stress, then that is what you will feel

and see. Until then, you must continue on,

playing your part, knowing better when you

remember (actually when the universe as you

remembers) and also knowing your experience

is evolving.

Since happening just happens and identification

changes as it happens, we should know all

doing is not ours to do. Yet we continues feeling

it is, as this is part of the play which is life. So

inside of this language, I say you do this, when

really I mean the creation at the point that is

the body and mind that the universe is

pretending to be you through. Language can get

convoluted when trying to explain this

perspective exactly, as can the understanding of the experience itself. Ultimately all is done by this creation. All happening is observed by the beingness that we all are, reduced to awareness -which is the way beingness experiences creation. Beyond and through it all, we, as being, experience our beingness.

I Do Not Exist and Neither Do You!

15   I Do Not Exist

Once you have made friends with the space

within, either through sitting in meditation on

your breath or heartbeat, or through just sitting

and watching the thoughts and focusing on the

space between them, allowing thought to flow

without attaching to it, then you recognize how

this silent, peaceful space feels. You become

intimately acquainted with it and begin to see it

is everywhere. Then you see you have the

choice of knowing this background as your

foreground whenever you choose. You also

begin to understand the statement "I do not

exist."

I as a person do not exist. The perspective of a person is a fantasy, an illusion, a part in the play of creation. Nothing less, nothing more. I as the beingness that is in, through and supporting all am all there is, ever. But this I is not an I, but just a feeling of being, a beingness. Not an I, so again, I does not exist.

You may say, so what if you don't exist; I do. If that is your feeling, then the entirety of the universal creation at the point that is you has decided that this information is not real or useful, and the part in the play that it will experience will not reference this concept again.

You may also say, so what if you don't exist and I don't exist. Here again, the universe has chosen to treat this information in this way at the space of your body and mind. With this thought comes different energy, different reactions, and eventually a different part in the play. There is no you to choose one reaction or the other, but the differences are clear, nonetheless. In one, the universe wants to have the same experience as always, while in the other the universe is wanting to open itself to something new. Happening will happen as it will. With the latter reaction, Creation is saying, let's see what experiences await me when I see the basis of life from a different, more expanded perspective. What can I experience as

beingness knowing itself inside of this play?

16   Creation As It Is

All things seen, all concepts believed, and
everything in-between is nothing more or less
than the sum total of the universe from its
beginning until this moment, moving exactly as
it will.

The initial movement has created all
subsequent motion and interaction and
complexity, and it is all as it should be. Nothing
happens that should not happen, from the
perspective of the whole (despite how very
wrong it may seem from the individual
perspective). Nothing that should happen

doesn't not happen. Creation is moving in complete control of all motion and emotion, and if it were supposed to be different, it would be.

In essence, the play has already been written and rehearsed, and we are watching the performance. As a member of the audience we can sit discontented, critical of each moment, enjoying nothing, or we can appreciate the play for what it is, as it is not ours and we have no say in changing it. Much like the screen cannot change the movie playing upon its surface, we cannot change the life appearing as our own. As much as we may wish it were different, or as much peace as we gather from knowing it, we cannot do anything differently, and we cannot

not do anything differently from how the

universe intends. Feeling trapped or free is the

universe's choice at the space of you at this

moment.

17   The End to Seeking

When we allow the individual mind to become
still, and when the universe chooses to
experience the totality of itself through this
point, then you experience your real body at
the point of your mind.

But the need for the universal consciousness to
experience itself as the universe through an
individual mind occurs fleetingly since it always
experiences itself through all minds anyway.
The small mind may yearn for this fantasy
realization, or moment of glory, but the whole
of creation already experiences it. Much like the

puppeteer is the consciousness behind all the movements of all the puppets, the beingness you are is the sustenance behind all creation. Most puppeteers do not use one puppet to control the others when putting on a show.

Don't get trapped awaiting an illusion that may never come. Instead accept your understanding and experiences, and value them as what is perfect for the universe at the point you call yourself. Believe in yourself and believe that your understanding is clear.

Looking for the next perfect description or just a little bit more information is a trap that seekers around the world have fallen into. There is always a guru who knows a little more, a master who can say it in just the right way to make the

heavens open up before us, we believe.

Much like waiting for that perfect someone to

love, we let one who is perfect-for-me pass us

by while we await a perfect person who does

not exist. Accept that you can know the truth,

and that there is nothing wrong with your

understanding. Right understanding has a

power of its own, and it will correct itself using

the mind as its tool, if you can allow it to do so.

It also never stands still, but is ever expanding,

growing and becoming deeper. Seeking can be a

lifelong addiction; be a finder ever developing

instead.

18   Keys to Living Beyond the Mind

The keys to living in the space beyond thought

are:

1.   Let go of the importance of thought.

        Stop believing each and every thought

        is important. This lets you live now,

        instead of living in your mind,

        cataloging every event. You don't watch

        a sunset and think oh wow, this is

        beautiful, this is almost as nice as the

        one I saw in California last year, or the

one I.... Instead, when you see a sunrise you have no thought. You feel it inside you as an amazing expression of your universal body.

You also do not fall into the traps that thinking creates, like worrying about the next moment (over which you have no control). You don't live in fantasies all day, but instead allow the moment to provide its own sublime enjoyment. You allow memory to be a tool, called upon as needed, instead of being an escape from facing things as they are.

So many uses of mind are like talking about the joys or fears of swimming, or

walking around the pool, or even
reminiscing about how much fun it was
to swim long ago, instead of just diving
into the pool right in front of you.

2.   Let go of the need to control your life.

Whereas before you thought you were
a person in a race known as life, now
you see that you are the track and the
stadium and the racers and the race
itself. You are intimately experiencing
one aspect of the race through one
racer, but this does not diminish the
fact that you are really it all. As all of
this, you do not need to win every time.
Or actually you do win every time, and

you lose every time too, but the need to
have the body you are most intimately
aware of win every time ceases. In each
moment you do the best that you can,
as you find out what the universe has in
store for you, and you appreciate the
whole spectacle of the race.

3. Let go of the need to judge and
    complain.

    Realize that a large majority of the
    noise of the mind is simply not agreeing
    with the way things are. This
    disagreeing takes the form of judging
    things to be bad, different, strange, or
    wrong, or it takes the form of

complaining about some event not being as our limited mind and perspective has decided it should be. Seeing this, we find that we can stop this incredibly foolish mental movement, and instead enjoy hours of peace and acceptance each day.

It's like we go to the movies to see a love story and then spend the entire two hours wanting to see a story filled with action or adventure or horror instead. Acceptance of being where you are, doing what you are doing, instead of complaining about a situation or judging it to be wrong is key to freeing yourself from unnecessary mental

noise.

Doing these three things everyday will take you

from a place where thought was the ruler to a

place where the space of stillness between

thought can be seen, appreciated, and

continually experienced.

19   Beingness

A final reminder of why I do not exist, and why

you don't exist either:

We are nothing but a feeling of being.

As much as we may want to be more, we are

not. As long as we have thought otherwise, we

were wrong. We are the universal field of being

that is felt in the mind as I. We have only the

universe as our true body, and only

consciousness as our mind.

At our essence we are nothing other than a

feeling. We are not a person with a body, not a

thinking mind, not a bundle of emotions even. We are the feeling behind it all; we are the stillness existing underneath when we let go of all the stuff happening on the surface.

Acceptance of the truth of our shared being allows the universe at the point where we experience life to be free. Knowing that your essence is being brings your completion.

Realizing yourself as no more and no less than being itself, the essence of all, grants a new, joyful perspective to life beyond anything your mind, or your previously misunderstood relation to existence could ever bring.

I do not exist; you do not exist.

We are existence.

We are beingness itself.

20   Reading List

If you liked this book, introduce others to

this perspective by giving it stars (5!) or

writing a review. Read other

recommended titles shown below.

Non Fiction:

I Don't Care: The Reality of Who You Are by G.

Tyler Wright

How to Become Enlightened in 12 Days by G.

Tyler Wright

Enlightenment Now: The Keys to Awakening by

G. Tyler Wright

How to Transform Your Life in 9 Days:

Awakening and Living Your Life Connected to

Being by G. Tyler Wright

Three Easy Steps to Enlightenment: Essential

Inner Shifts for Realizing the Self by G. Tyler

Wright

The Happy Mom's Guide: Reducing Stress in

Your Life- 10 Days to Freedom by G. Tyler

Wright

How to Find Your Royal Ancestry for Free in Less

Than 14 Days by Gregory Wright

Transcendent Fiction:

The first full length novel in the Gray Soul Saga

Gray Soul: An Extraordinary Spiritual Journey by

Gregory Wright

The Game's On: Play to Stay Alive by Gregory

Wright

Parallel Love by Gregory Wright

Alarm Yourself by Gregory Wright

Beware the Haze in the Distance by Greg Wright

Surfin' to the End of the World by Greg Wright

Printed in Great Britain
by Amazon

64280600R00061